Chains of Silence

Unveiling Foucault's Disciplinary Power

The Curious Philosopher

Copyright Page

Disclaimer

The views and opinions expressed in this book are those of the author(s) and do not necessarily reflect the official policy or position of any other agency, organization, employer, or company. The contents of this book are for informational and educational purposes only and are not intended to serve as professional advice, diagnosis, or treatment.

The information provided in this book is believed to be accurate and reliable as of the date of publication. However, it may include some errors or inaccuracies, and no warranty or guarantee is provided regarding the accuracy, timeliness, or applicability of the content.

Readers are encouraged to consult with professional philosophers, educators, or other qualified professionals where appropriate for personalized advice. The author(s) and publisher shall not be liable for any loss, damage, or harm caused or alleged to be caused, directly or indirectly, by the information or ideas contained, suggested, or referenced in this book.

By reading this book, the reader acknowledges and agrees that they are solely responsible for how they interpret and apply the information contained herein.

This book may also include references to other works, studies, and sources. These references are provided for further reading and exploration and do not imply endorsement or validation of the specific theories, viewpoints, or interpretations presented in those works.

Chapter 1: Unveiling the Unseen: Foucault and the Power That Shapes Us

In the heart of France, amidst the chaos of post-World War II, emerged a thinker, Michel Foucault, whose ideas would transcend borders and generations. Born in 1926, this historian and philosopher dived deep into the realms of power, knowledge, and social institutions, offering a lens through which we could see the invisible forces shaping our lives. His intellectual journey birthed a concept that remains as relevant today as it was then - the concept of disciplinary power.

At its core, Foucault's idea of disciplinary power is about the unseen forces that guide our behavior in society. It's not just about a king, a president, or a boss exerting power. It's about a much subtler form of control that's woven into the fabric of our everyday lives. Picture a school, for example. Without a second thought, children line up in neat rows, follow a bell's schedule, and adhere to a set of rules that govern everything from how they dress to how they interact with others. This, in a nutshell, is disciplinary power at work. It's a form of power that's not wielded with a sword, but with a timetable, a rulebook, a dress code.

But why should we care about a theory birthed in the corridors of French academia decades ago? Well, because Foucault's concept of disciplinary power is not confined to the pages of dusty old books; it's at play in our schools, workplaces, hospitals, and even in our own behaviors and thoughts. When we adhere to social norms, when we monitor our own behavior fearing judgment or punishment, when we strive to fit into boxes crafted by society, we are dancing to the tunes of disciplinary power.

In today's world, the tentacles of disciplinary power stretch far and wide. With the advent of technology, the gaze of surveillance extends beyond the physical into the digital, tracking our every move, shaping our behaviors even when we think we are free from scrutiny. Disciplinary power molds us, often without our conscious realization.

This exploration isn't meant to paint a gloomy picture, but to awaken awareness. By understanding the forces at play, we are better equipped to navigate the maze of social expectations and norms, to question the unseen hands that guide us, and to carve our own path in a world of unseen control.

As we delve deeper into Foucault's world in the coming chapters, we will unfold the layers of disciplinary power, scrutinize its mechanisms, and explore its manifestations in various institutions. This journey will not only unveil the often invisible structures of power but also prompt a reflection on how we, as individuals and communities, can engage with, challenge, and perhaps reshape the forces that silently steer our lives.

As you turn the pages, you may find yourself looking at the world, and your place in it, through a new lens, one that unveils the subtle strings of power that orchestrate the dance of society. So, shall we dance?

Chapter 2: The Silent Shift: The Rise of Disciplinary Power Through Ages

Once upon a time, power was straightforward. It was about kings and queens, lords and ladies, wielding control over the masses. It was a tale of thrones, where those atop dictated the rules, and those below obeyed, or faced the wrath. This was the pre-modern era, where the chains of control were visible, tangible, and often, brutal.

But as the pages of history turned, a subtle shift began to brew. The dawn of the modern era brought with it a new kind of power, one that was less about crowns and more about codes, less about thrones and more about norms. This was the birth of disciplinary power, a silent force that didn't rule with an iron fist, but with a gentle nudge, a whisper in the hallways of society, a seemingly benign guideline that shaped the actions and thoughts of individuals. It was no longer just about the mighty king or the stern lord; it was about institutions, rules, and routines that orchestrated the behavior of the masses.

This shift didn't happen in isolation. The gears of the industrial revolution began to turn, setting the stage for a new world. Factories replaced fields, machines replaced men, and amidst this mechanical melody, disciplinary power found its rhythm. As people flocked to work in the newly birthed factories, a new form of control took center stage. It was no longer enough to merely obey the lord; now, one had to adhere to the ticking clock, the factory whistle, the regimented routine.

The emergence of modern institutions further fueled this shift. Schools, hospitals, prisons, and military establishments became arenas where disciplinary power danced its subtle dance. In schools, it was about the bell that signaled the start and end of lessons, the rules that dictated every aspect of student life. In hospitals, it was about the protocols that governed patient care, the hierarchies that structured interactions. In prisons and military establishments, it was about the routines that regimented life, the disciplines that defined behavior.

The role of industrialization was akin to a composer creating a melody for disciplinary power to dance to. It created a structured, organized, and regimented society, where the norms and routines governed the day, where the individual was but a cog in the vast machinery of modern life.

As the factories hummed and the schools bells rang, as the hospital wards bustled and the prison gates clanged, the tendrils of disciplinary power wove their way into the fabric of society, silently, steadily, shaping the contours of modern life. The king's scepter was replaced by the factory manager's clock, the lord's decree by the school's rulebook, the gallows by the prison cell.

The story of disciplinary power is not just a tale of a bygone era, but a narrative that continues to unfold, a silent script that continues to shape our lives in ways we often overlook. As we journey further into this narrative, we'll explore the mechanisms through which disciplinary power operates, and how it manifests in the various institutions that dot the landscape of modern life.

This chapter opens the door to a world where power is not just about the mighty, but about the many, where control is not wielded with a sword, but with a subtle, silent script that orchestrates the rhythm of modern life.

Chapter 3: The Invisible Strings: How Disciplinary Power Pulls the Puppet

As we delve into the mechanisms of disciplinary power, we unravel the invisible strings that pull at the puppetry of our daily lives. Picture a vast theatre, where society plays out its script, and behind the scenes, three puppeteers—Surveillance, Normalization, and Examination—maneuver the strings.

Let's step into the first act: Surveillance. Imagine a guard tower in the middle of a courtyard, from where the guard can see every cell, but the inmates can't see the guard. This was an idea called Panopticism, coined by our philosopher, Michel Foucault, inspired by a design by Jeremy Bentham. But it's not just about a physical tower and a guard; it's about the idea that someone could be watching. This notion nudges individuals to behave in certain ways, just by the mere possibility of being observed.

Now, transition this thought into the digital age. Cameras on every street corner, data being collected with each click online, our actions being tracked, analyzed, and stored. The modern world has taken

Panopticism to a level beyond what Bentham or Foucault could have envisioned. The tower is now in the cloud, the guard replaced by algorithms, yet the essence remains: we act as if we are being watched, because, well, we are.

Now, onto the second act: Normalization. It's about setting a 'standard', a 'norm' that individuals are expected to adhere to. Think about the first day of school, the uniforms, the rules of conduct, the grading system. These norms shape our behavior, our desires to fit in, to be 'normal'. Schools play a pivotal role here, churning out individuals who adhere to societal norms, who strive for the grades, the accolades, the approval.

But it's not just about schools, it's about the unspoken rules that govern our behavior in social settings, at work, even at home. Normalization is the puppeteer that ensures the puppet dances to the tune of societal expectations, often without questioning who composed the tune in the first place.

Lastly, we step into the third act: Examination. It's about evaluating, categorizing, and defining individuals based on certain criteria. Recall the nerve-wracking feeling of exams, of being judged, labeled, and placed into boxes—'smart', 'average', 'below average'. Beyond schools, think about medical check-ups, psychological evaluations, where individuals are assessed, diagnosed, and often, stigmatized. Examination sets the stage for individuals to be managed, controlled, and often, corrected to fit into societal molds.

As the curtains close on this chapter, we are left with a lingering thought. The puppeteers of disciplinary power—Surveillance, Normalization, and Examination—operate in the shadows, yet their strings pull at the core of our being, shaping our actions, our thoughts, even our desires. The theatre of society goes on, with each individual playing their part, often oblivious to the invisible strings that guide their dance. Yet, as we shall see in the chapters to come, these strings can be seen, felt, and perhaps, even snipped, setting the stage for a new script, a new dance, a new narrative of power and freedom.

Chapter 4: The Silent Architects: Institutions and the Blueprint of Control

Picture society as a grand building, with various rooms each serving a unique purpose. In this architectural marvel, institutions act as the silent architects, designing the blueprint of control, sketching the outlines of disciplinary power. Let's venture into these rooms and decipher the designs etched by the architects.

First, we step into the somber halls of Prisons. These are more than mere enclosures of brick and mortar; they are emblematic of disciplinary power in its rawest form. Within these walls, every action is monitored, every movement regulated. The layout is meticulous, designed to observe, to categorize, to reform. The prison, in essence, embodies the essence of control, striving to mold individuals into socially acceptable molds.

Now, we wander into the bustling corridors of Schools. Here, the architecture of control is subtle, yet profound. The ringing bells, the structured timetable, the grading system; all are instruments tuning the behavior of students. Schools sketch the primary outlines of disciplinary power, instilling norms, shaping minds, preparing individuals for the larger societal structure.

As we stroll further, we enter the sanitized aisles of Hospitals. Here, the scent of disinfectants mingles with the essence of control. The hierarchy among medical staff, the protocols governing patient care, the meticulous documentation; all are strokes of disciplinary power. Hospitals are realms where care and control dance a delicate duet, where the quest for health navigates the maze of structured protocols.

Lastly, we march into the disciplined realms of the Military. Amidst the cadence of marching boots, the essence of disciplinary power resonates loudly. The rigid hierarchy, the regimented routine, the unyielding discipline; all are hallmarks of control, crafting individuals into cohesive units, ready to act at the command.

As we step out of this architectural marvel, we carry with us a nuanced understanding of how institutions, the silent architects, craft the blueprint of disciplinary power. They sketch the outlines, lay down the rules, and set the stage for the grand play of society. Yet, within this design, there lies the potential for change, for re-sketching the outlines, for re-imagining the architecture. The rooms can be reshaped, the blueprint redrawn, opening doors to new realms of thought, action, and societal structure.

In the subsequent chapters, we will delve deeper into the dialogues and daily practices that further engrave the lines of disciplinary power, and explore the strokes of resistance that dare to sketch a new design in this grand architectural narrative of society. Our journey through the rooms of disciplinary power is but a preamble to the larger exploration of how we, as individuals and communities, interact with, challenge, and perhaps, reshape the silent sketches of control etched by the architects of society.

Chapter 5: The Silent Script: Discourses and Daily Dances

In the grand narrative of society, discourses and practices are the script and choreography guiding our daily dances. They are the dialogues we engage in and the steps we follow, often subconsciously, as we waltz through the routine of life. In this chapter, we'll delve into the nuanced choreography crafted by language and daily practices, and how they subtly steer the course of our societal ballet.

First on stage is Language and Discourse. Imagine language as the scriptwriter, sketching the dialogues of societal interactions. The words we use, the terms we coin, the labels we attach, all play a pivotal role in reinforcing or challenging the existing power structures. For instance, how we talk about gender, race, or class can either perpetuate stereotypes or pave the way for inclusivity. The script of language is not merely a set of words; it's a reflection of societal norms and power dynamics.

Now, let's delve deeper into the act of creating 'truth' through discourse. Truth isn't an absolute entity but a construct shaped by the dominant dialogues. For instance, what is deemed as 'normal' or 'abnormal' is often a product of prevailing discourses. The medical discourse, for example, shapes our understanding of health and illness, while the legal discourse defines what's right and wrong. These discourses, shaped by the power structures, in turn, shape our perception of truth, coloring the lens through which we view the world.

Next on stage are Everyday Practices, the choreography guiding our daily dances. Rituals and routines, from the morning coffee to the evening news, are the steps we follow, often without a second thought. They provide a sense of order, a rhythm to our chaotic lives. Yet, they also embody the subtle nudges of disciplinary power, guiding our actions along the lines of societal expectations.

Now, let's twirl into the realm of Social Interactions and Relationships. Every handshake, every conversation, every social gathering is a dance of power dynamics. The way we interact with our peers, our superiors, our subordinates, all are shaped by the unwritten rules of society. These interactions, in turn, reinforce or challenge the established power structures, either keeping the choreography intact or introducing new steps into the societal dance.

As the curtain falls on this chapter, we are left with a thought-provoking realization. The script of discourses and the choreography of daily practices are not merely passive backdrops; they are active players in the grand narrative of society, scripting the dialogues and sketching the steps of our daily dances. Yet, the script can be rewritten, the choreography reimagined, as we, the actors, gain awareness of the silent strings pulling at the puppetry of our lives. In the chapters to come, we will explore the avenues of resistance and the potential to choreograph a new dance, a dance of awareness, empowerment, and transformation.

Chapter 6: Breaking Free: The Dance of Resistance and Counter-conduct

As we've journeyed through the corridors of disciplinary power, we've witnessed the silent strings that govern our actions and mold our societies. Yet, amidst this seemingly rigid choreography, there lies a potential for a different kind of dance, a dance of resistance and counter-conduct. In this chapter, we'll explore the rhythm of resistance, the choreography of counter-conduct, and the potential for crafting a new narrative of emancipation and social change.

First, let's delve into Foucault's idea of counter-conduct. Imagine a dancer on stage, moving against the rhythm, breaking free from the choreographed steps to create a new dance. This is what Foucault referred to as counter-conduct, the act of moving against the currents of disciplinary power, challenging the established choreography, and introducing new steps into the societal dance. It's about questioning the script, challenging the norms, and crafting a new narrative that challenges the established order.

Now, let's look at some real-life examples of resistance to disciplinary power. Think of the Civil Rights Movement, where individuals rallied against racial discrimination, challenging the entrenched power structures. Or consider the feminist movement, where women and allies questioned and resisted the traditional gender roles and norms. These movements represent a collective dance of resistance, where individuals came together to challenge the disciplinary power and carve out a new choreography of social interactions and justice.

Lastly, let's explore the potential for emancipation and social change. The dance of resistance and counter-conduct doesn't merely challenge the existing choreography; it opens up a space for crafting a new narrative, for redefining the norms, and for envisioning a society where the strings of disciplinary power are replaced by threads of empowerment, equality, and justice. It's about moving from a scripted dance to an improvised rhythm where individuals and communities have the agency to define their own choreography, free from the rigid routines of disciplinary power.

As we conclude this chapter, we are left with a sense of hope and a vision of a new societal choreography. The dance of resistance and counter-conduct is not merely an act of defiance; it's a pathway towards crafting a new narrative, towards a society where the rhythm of disciplinary power is replaced by the melody of emancipation and social justice. Our exploration doesn't end here; as we delve into the critiques and reflections in the chapters to come, we continue to unravel the layers of disciplinary power and the potential for crafting a new narrative of societal interaction and empowerment.

Chapter 7: Beyond the Veil: Critiques and Conversations Around Foucault's Concept

As we meander through the rich landscape of Foucault's ideas, it's imperative to also venture into the realms of critique and conversation that surround his concept of disciplinary power. This chapter aims to shed light on the debates within social theory and scrutinize the applicability of Foucault's ideas in our contemporary global tapestry.

Let's first dive into the pool of Debates within Social Theory. Like any profound theory, Foucault's concept has stirred a pot of diverse opinions and interpretations among scholars. Some argue that his focus on power dynamics overlooks other crucial societal factors like economic conditions or individual agency. Others debate on Foucault's portrayal of power as somewhat omnipresent, which they argue, might paint a somewhat deterministic picture, leaving little room for resistance and change. These debates are not merely academic jousts; they shape the way we understand, engage with, and possibly, challenge or extend Foucault's ideas.

Now, let's traverse into the terrain of Applicability and Relevance in Contemporary Global Contexts. The world is a vast mosaic of cultures, traditions, and socio-political setups. How does Foucault's concept of disciplinary power resonate in this diverse global arena? For instance, in authoritarian regimes, the exercise of power may be more overt and coercive, while in democracies, the subtle strings of disciplinary power might resonate more. Similarly, in the digital age, the surveillance aspect of disciplinary power takes a new, perhaps more pervasive form. Foucault's idea, born in a specific socio-political context, does it stretch across the diverse global stage? Or does it require a re-tuning to resonate with different societal rhythms?

As we step back, the critiques and conversations around Foucault's concept invite us to look beyond the veil, to engage with the theory critically, to question, to debate, and to reflect. They encourage us not to take the theory at face value, but to dissect it, to explore its nuances, its strengths, and its limitations. They beckon us to ponder on how the concept of disciplinary power fits into our global narrative, and how it can be extended, refined, or possibly, challenged to better understand and navigate the complex web of societal dynamics.

As we draw the curtains on this chapter, we are left with more questions, a broader perspective, and a richer understanding of the myriad dimensions that surround Foucault's concept of disciplinary power. Our exploration is a journey, one that doesn't end, but rather, deepens with every critique, every conversation, and every reflection we engage in. As we move forward, these critiques and conversations are the stepping stones that guide our way, that challenge our understanding, and that enrich our intellectual voyage through the realms of disciplinary power and beyond.

Chapter 8: Reflections in the Mirror: The Enduring Relevance of Foucault's Disciplinary Power

As we step into the concluding chapter of our exploration, let's pause for a moment, like a traveler at the end of a journey, to reflect on the paths traversed and the horizons expanded. Our expedition through the realms of Foucault's concept of disciplinary power has been akin to peeling layers off an onion, revealing the nuanced interplay of invisible forces shaping our actions, institutions, and societal structures.

Recapitulating the key points, we delved into the intricacies of surveillance, normalization, and examination as the mechanisms of disciplinary power. We explored how institutions like prisons, schools, hospitals, and the military serve as the architects of this silent control. We witnessed the script of language and daily practices that further engrave the lines of disciplinary power into our societal fabric. And we danced through the rhythm of resistance and counter-conduct, exploring the potential for carving out a new narrative of social interaction and empowerment.

As we hold the mirror of reflection to the concept of disciplinary power, its enduring relevance in our contemporary world becomes evidently clear. In a digital era where surveillance has transcended into virtual realms, where algorithms and data analytics exert a new form of control, Foucault's ideas ring truer than ever. The choreography of societal norms and practices continues to shape our daily interactions, our self-identity, and our relationships with others.

Moreover, the global resonance of disciplinary power amidst diverse political, cultural, and socio-economic contexts underscores its profound relevance. The dance of disciplinary power transcends borders, manifesting in nuanced ways across the global stage, influencing not just individuals but entire communities and nations.

The beauty of Foucault's concept lies in its ability to unveil the often invisible threads of control, empowering us with the awareness to recognize, question, and possibly, redefine the choreography of power in our lives and in our societies. It beckons us to continue the dialogue, to challenge the norms, and to engage in a collective dance towards a more aware, empowered, and just society.

Our exploration doesn't end here; rather, it opens up avenues for further inquiry, reflection, and action. The pages may conclude, but the narrative continues, inviting each one of us to engage with, reflect upon, and contribute to the evolving discourse around power, control, and emancipation.

As we close this chapter, let's carry forth the essence of Foucault's ideas into our daily dialogues, into our societal engagements, and into our collective consciousness. May the exploration of disciplinary power serve as a catalyst for deeper understanding, critical inquiry, and constructive action in our shared journey towards a more equitable and empowered society.

About The Curious Philosopher

Welcome to The Curious Philosopher, your dedicated platform for diving deep into the world of philosophy. We are more than just a YouTube channel or a book publisher. We are a beacon of enlightenment, making complex philosophical concepts accessible and engaging for all.

Our YouTube channel is a rich repository of philosophy made simple. We take the profound and often complex ideas from the world of philosophy and break them down into digestible, easy-to-understand content. From the ancient wisdom of Socrates to the existentialist thoughts of Sartre, we cover a broad spectrum of philosophical schools and thoughts, making philosophy accessible to everyone, regardless of their background or prior knowledge.

As a book publisher, we take the same approach, transforming intricate philosophical theories into comprehensible narratives. Our books are not just collections of words, but vessels of wisdom that make philosophy approachable and relatable. We believe that philosophy should not be confined to academic circles, but should be available to all who seek to understand the world and their place in it.

At The Curious Philosopher, we believe in the power of curiosity and the pursuit of knowledge. We are here to stoke the fires of your curiosity, to guide you on your intellectual journey, and to help you navigate the fascinating world of philosophy.

If you are someone who is not afraid to question, to explore, and to learn, then you are in the right place. Join us on this journey of exploration, as we make philosophy easy to understand, one concept at a time.

Be sure to visit our Youtube channel at:

https://www.curiousphilosopher.com/youtube

You can also visit us on the web at

https://www.curiousphilosopher.com

Welcome to The Curious Philosopher. Stay curious. Stay enlightened.

www.ingramcontent.com/pod-product-compliance
Lightning Source LLC
Chambersburg PA
CBHW060913260726
48661CB00008B/3617